Routes to Writing

PROGRAMME GUIDE

Author and Series Editor: **Amanda George**
Series Advisers: **Monica Hughes** *and* **Isabel Macdonald**

Contents

OXFORD
UNIVERSITY PRESS

What is Routes to Writing?

Routes to Writing is an exciting writing programme for children aged 4–7 which provides you with all the support you need to help your children to develop as confident, independent writers.

How does Routes to Writing work?

Routes to Writing covers all the fiction and non-fiction text types required at Key Stage 1/P1–3. It uses an innovative mixture of both shared and guided writing to give your children the chance to gain a real understanding of the way each text type works. It is organised into units of work which match the range of text types suggested by the National Literacy Strategy. Within each unit, the programme provides resources for shared writing sessions and differentiated guided writing sessions.

What does Routes to Writing have to offer?

Routes to Writing provides:

A **Big Book** for each Year, containing
- Whole texts for use in shared writing sessions
- The key features of each text type highlighted for use in Talk for Writing
- Specially written, child-friendly models for writing

A **Pupil Book** for each unit, containing
- 2 differentiated whole texts, so you can tailor guided writing sessions to your children's needs
- The key features of each text type highlighted to consolidate understanding
- Carefully levelled texts which are ideal models for children's own writing

Easy-to-use **Teaching Notes**, containing
- Comprehensive prompts and ideas for use in shared, guided and independent writing
- A comprehensive overview of the key features of each text type
- Practical ideas for purposeful stimulus sessions
- Clear and helpful advice on planning and assessment

1 **CD-ROM** for each Year, containing
- Complete manipulable versions of the big book texts for use with interactive whiteboards
- Photocopy masters in PDF format, so you can print them out anywhere
- A video showing you how to get the most out of the scheme.

This **Programme Guide** provides you with an overview of how the programme works. It also includes charts showing coverage of NLS objectives and the progression of writing outcomes, and levelling charts to show you how the pupil books are differentiated and which key features of each type are being used. It also contains a correlation to the Scottish 5–14 Guidelines, and a glossary of writing terminology.

Please see the programme chart on pages 4–5.

Using a unit of work

Each pack of *Pupil Books* is accompanied by a short *Teaching Notes* book which provides specific support and guidance for the text type covered in both the *Pupil Books* and the *Big Book*. Within each *Teaching Notes*, you will find support for the following structure of work.

- *Pre-writing and stimulus activities* The *Teaching Notes* provide you with activities which are designed to provide a context for the children, and to develop key ideas and core vocabulary prior to writing.
- *Shared writing sessions* The *Big Book* provides a complete text to use as a model in both shared reading and writing. There is support for three shared writing sessions for each unit. These sessions have clearly identified objectives and provide opportunities for you to develop specific aspects of writing related to a particular text type.
- *Guided writing sessions* The *Pupil Book* for each unit includes two whole examples of the same text type as the *Big Book*. These texts are differentiated (one easier and one harder) for use with your different ability groups. This enables you to consolidate and extend the key concepts introduced in the shared sessions and this provides a crucial bridge between shared and independent writing. The *Teaching Notes* include two writing frames or photocopy masters (PCMs) for use with each pupil book text.
- *Independent activities* The *Teaching Notes* provide you with suggestions for independent writing activities related to the unit of work (some have PCMs provided).
- *Plenary or session summary* The *Teaching Notes* provide suggestions for key questions which can be used in the plenary, or within a separate session summary.

When do I use a unit – how long will it take?

We would suggest that you use a unit over one or two weeks. However, the programme has been designed to be very flexible, and you can use the material as appropriate within the needs of your class. You can also use the *Pupil Books* as an add-on to any existing Big Book writing programme you may already own.

A suggested route is provided in each *Teaching Notes* on page 4. Whilst we would strongly recommend that you follow the progression of shared writing leading to guided writing, which in turn leads to independent writing, the way you use the programme can be adapted to suit the abilities of your class.

Routes to Writing

| | Big Books | Pupil's Books Packs.. |

3 examples of every text type give children the exposure they need in order to write successfully.

Reception / P1

Big Books contain one complete example for every text type.

Pupil's Books contain two differentiated examples of a text type so you can tailor your sessions.

One Teaching Notes per Unit, with all the support you need for shared, guided and independent writing

ISBN 0 19 845307 8

UNIT 1 — Nursery Rhymes

UNIT 2 — Information Books

ISBN 0 19 845295 0

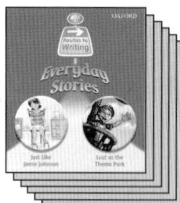

ISBN 0 19 845296 9

Year 1 / P2

Shared writing sessions help develop speaking and listening skills.

ISBN 0 19 845327 2

UNIT 1 Everyday Stories	UNIT 2 Instructions	UNIT 3 Signs and Labels	UNIT 4 Fairy Tales
ISBN 0 19 845309 4	ISBN 0 19 845310 8	ISBN 0 19 845311 6	ISBN 0 19 845312 4

Year 2 / P3

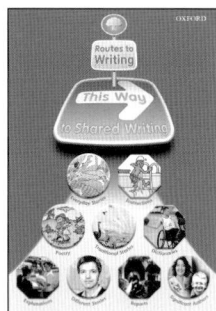

ISBN 0 19 845349 3

UNIT 1 Everyday Stories	UNIT 2 Instructions	UNIT 3 Poetry	UNIT 4 Traditional Stories
ISBN 0 19 845329 9	ISBN 0 19 845330 2	ISBN 0 19 845331 0	ISBN 0 19 845332 9

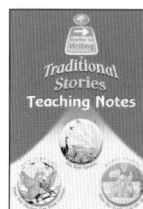

...including Teaching Notes

UNIT 3	UNIT 4	UNIT 5	UNIT 6
Modern Rhymes	Patterned Stories	Recounts	Traditional Stories

ISBN 0 19 845308 6

| ISBN 0 19 845297 7 | ISBN 0 19 845298 5 | ISBN 0 19 845299 3 | ISBN 0 19 845300 0 |

Complete Big Book texts for use on interactive whiteboards – and much more!

UNIT 5	UNIT 6	UNIT 7	UNIT 8	UNIT 9
Stories from Around the World	Reports	Fantasy Stories	Poetry	Recounts

ISBN 0 19 845328 0

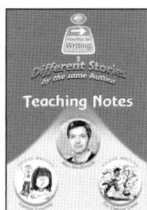

| ISBN 0 19 845313 2 | ISBN 0 19 845314 0 | ISBN 0 19 845315 9 | ISBN 0 19 845316 7 | ISBN 0 19 845317 5 |

UNIT 5	UNIT 6	UNIT 7	UNIT 8	UNIT 9
Dictionaries	Explanations	Different Stories by the Same Author	Reports	Stories by Significant Authors

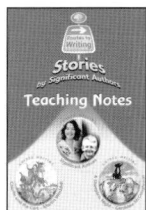

ISBN 0 19 845350 7

| ISBN 0 19 845338 8 | ISBN 0 19 845335 3 | ISBN 0 19 845336 1 | ISBN 0 19 845339 6 | ISBN 0 19 845337 X |

The teaching of writing is a complex task. There are many aspects of writing which need to be taught thoroughly and systematically before you can expect children to become successful independent writers.

The differences between spoken and written language

There are three key factors which differentiate spoken and written language.

- **Text cohesion** This refers to the way in which text is joined together and flows logically. It is crucial to help children to develop a logical sequence of ideas and also to use specific techniques to link phrases and sentences together.
- **Sentence construction and punctuation** Another key factor in ensuring successful writing is putting words together in coherent sentences. In addition, children need to use correct punctuation to demarcate these sentences.
- **Word choice and modification** You also need to help children develop a wide vocabulary. They need to know how to use this vocabulary to add interest, clarify meaning and adapt their writing to different audiences and purposes.

Routes to Writing provides you with the resources and support to develop all three of these aspects of writing with the children through carefully planned shared and guided writing sessions.

Writing for different purposes

Children also need to learn to adapt their writing for different purposes and audiences. For example, they need to know that writing a story is very different from writing a report or a poem. There are certain conventions which need to be used, depending on the type of writing (or text type).

Each text type has specific 'rules' which need to be adhered to. *Routes to Writing* will help you to uncover and explore these elements with the children – and show them how to use them to create their own successful pieces of writing. The Overview Chart in the *Teaching Notes* explains the different purposes, organisational and language features for each text type. The Teaching Focus Chart then demonstrates ways in which you can introduce and develop this knowledge with your children.

Transcriptional skills

The primary focus of *Routes to Writing* is to support the teaching of compositional skills. This is because it is key to successful writing, and needs specific and thorough attention. Transcriptional skills (focusing on handwriting and spelling) are also crucial, and children should have specific times when this is the focus of their work.

You should take opportunities to model the application of phonic knowledge and correct letter formation within the context of shared writing sessions. It is important, however, to focus on one thing at a time. Children may, for example, only produce one label or sentence initially, not in perfect handwriting – the important thing to assess is whether they have achieved the relevant focus you have set out.

THE ROUTE TO SUCCESSFUL WRITING

To provide children with the best chances of success with their writing, we recommend you take them carefully through a teaching sequence which leads them from being wholly dependent on the teacher, to being able to do it for themselves.

Shared reading

It is important to provide children with a clear model for their writing. Using this model text, you can analyse and discuss the key features of a text type – thus providing children with some clear pointers for their own writing. For example, in order to write a recount, children need to know that it should be written in the first or third person and in the past tense.

The models of text provided in the *Big Books* include all the key features of each particular text type (selected ones are highlighted in bold or in colour), with guidance provided in the *Teaching Notes* on which points to bring out. You can also use the stimulus activities provided in the *Teaching Notes* for pre-writing sessions, to introduce any relevant concepts and vocabulary.

Shared writing

Talk for writing This allows you and the children to plan what you are going to write together and to 'get it right' before writing it down. It shows children how to clarify and refine their ideas before they start and will help to ensure that the writing is successful.

- **Teacher demonstration** (*"I'll show you."*) This is where you can demonstrate how a piece of writing can be done, including revisiting your ideas.
- **Teacher scribe** (*"Let's do it together."*) This is an opportunity for the children to have opportunities to develop writing ideas with you there for support. You can write down their ideas and help them to refine their thoughts.
- **Supported composition** (*"Now you have a go."*) This is a chance for children to 'have a go' at writing, but, again, with you there for support. It also allows you to see how well prepared children are to undertake any guided or independent writing tasks. (Please see page 8 for further detail on shared writing.)

Guided writing (*"You do it and I'll hold your hand."*)

This is the crucial step between shared and independent writing. The responsibility for the writing is handed over to the child, but you, the teacher, are still there to support and guide them as they write. It provides an essential opportunity for you to intervene at the point of writing, rather than waiting until the child has completed their writing and then pointing out where they went wrong! (Please see page 9 for further detail on guided writing.)

Evaluation

There are opportunities built throughout *Routes to Writing* which allow children to share and evaluate their writing. Children should make judgements about the success of their writing against key criteria, which you can establish at the beginning of the teaching sequence.

Effective shared writing is a very powerful tool. It enables you to show children how writers really write and to uncover some of the hidden aspects of the writing process.

Key features of shared writing

The key aspects of shared writing which are used in *Routes to Writing* are:

- **Talk for writing** It is important to clarify the ideas and the structure of the writing before you start writing. This can be done through discussion and rehearsal of sentences.

- **Teacher demonstration** (*"I'll show you."*) This is where you, the teacher, model how to construct a piece of writing, focusing on a specific objective. You should 'think out loud' during the writing, to show children how and why the writing is constructed in a particular way.

- **Teacher scribe** (*"Let's do it together."*) During this, you can ask for suggestions and contributions from the children and write them down on the board. You may need to refine the children's responses or to refocus them on the particular objective that is being developed.

- **Supported composition** (*"Now you have a go."*) The children can use individual whiteboards during this part of the session, working individually or in pairs. Alternatively, you could ask selected children to come up and write directly on your board. The children should write a short amount of focused text, based on your model. You will then be able to make an instant assessment of children's understanding of key concepts and their ability to tackle writing independently.

Techniques to use in shared writing

During each shared writing session there are a number of techniques you can model.

- **Oral rehearsal** Model for the children how to say the sentence out loud (often two or three times). This shows them how you can refine a sentence before writing it down. You should demonstrate for the children why you make any changes in writing and how word choices may be improved during oral rehearsal to create more impact.

- **Regular re-reading** It is important that children see that you do not have to wait until a piece of writing is complete before re-reading it to check that it makes sense, and that the writing flows well. You need to model re-reading constantly throughout a piece of writing.

- **Encouraging the automatic use of punctuation** There will be some sessions which focus specifically on the correct use of punctuation. During other sessions, it is important that the teacher models and explains where the appropriate punctuation should be included and why.

- **Deliberate mistakes** Occasionally you may find that it is beneficial to make a deliberate error in your writing. This will hold children's attention (they will be very quick to correct you!) and also enable you to focus on common errors related to the specific objective being taught.

- **Using writing frames** In the *Routes to Writing CD-ROMS*, you will find a specific writing frame for each unit, for use in shared writing. These range from lines to help you organise lists of rhyming words, to spidergrams. You can use these to help organise and plan your writing and model this for the children.

Guided writing is the key step between shared and independent writing. During guided writing sessions you have the opportunity to work with a small group of children and focus on very specific aspects of their writing development. This focus means that children can concentrate on one element of their writing – instead of trying to focus on all the complexities of creating a piece of writing at the same time – and develop very clear ideas about how they should be writing.

It is therefore important that, in guided sessions, children are grouped according to their ability level in writing. Whilst whole class shared writing sessions are an invaluable part of the teaching sequence, it is inevitable that children in every class will be working at different levels. In moving straight from shared to independent writing, there is therefore a danger that both lower and higher ability children will not progress successfully. In guided writing, children of similar abilities can work on improving similar aspects of their writing. *Routes to Writing* offers support and guidance not just for whole class sessions, but also for these all-important guided sessions.

The differentiated Pupil Books

As stated on page 3 of this Guide, there is one *Pupil Book* for each unit. Within this *Pupil Book*, there are two whole examples of the same text type as the *Big Book*.

- **The first text** is easier to read and enables the teacher to consolidate key concepts taught in the shared session with a lower ability group. This enables you to consolidate and extend the key concepts that have been introduced in the shared sessions.
- **The second text** has been designed for higher ability children, allowing you to extend and refine those key concepts with them.

These *Pupil Books* have been specifically designed to support teachers and children with unpicking the writing process. They provide clear, child-friendly models for writing, with carefully chosen subject matter and form to enable children to quickly imagine how they could write their own version. Key features of each text type are also sometimes highlighted in bold, or another colour, to help children remember them.

The easier text, whilst still presenting a clear model, provides a simple example with limited features which children should be able to identify and use in their own writing. The more difficult text presents the same text type, but with more of the key features and sometimes more complex elements which more able children will be able to recreate in their own writing.

The *Teaching Notes* provide two lesson plans for each of these two levels of guided writing.

- **The first lesson plan** outlines a session where children explore and discuss the key writing features of the text type.
- **The second lesson plan** encourages children to use the text as a model for their own writing.

For each of these two lessons, a writing frame or photocopiable master is provided to support children with their written work. As the children write, you should intervene as appropriate and support individual children as they complete their writing.

RECEPTION/P1 Key Objectives and Writing Outcomes

Text types	Objectives	Writing outcomes
UNIT 1 **Nursery Rhymes** **BB:** Humpty Dumpty/One, Two, Buckle my Shoe **PB:** Ring-a-Ring-a-Roses **PB:** Polly Puts the Kettle On	**To recognise a pattern** **To recognise and use alliteration** T10 to re-read and recite stories and rhymes with predictable and repeated patterns and experiment with similar rhyming patterns T12b to write their own names T12e to experiment with writing and recognise how their own version matches and differs from conventional versions T13 to think about and discuss what they want to write ahead of writing it	**SW:** write new rhyming couplets; new rhymes and simple sentences; speech bubble for Humpty Dumpty. **GW:** write new actions for rhyme; a sentence about the story; speech bubbles; sentences using the same pattern.
UNIT 2 **Information Books** **BB:** Floppy's Book of Dogs **PB:** Colours **PB:** Inside a Fruit	**To know that information books are different from stories** T1b that words can be written down to be read again for a wide range of purposes T1c to understand and use correctly terms about books T1a to understand that writing can be used for a range of purposes T1c to distinguish between writing and drawing in books and in own work T1d to understand how writing is formed directionally, a word at a time T2c to write labels or captions for pictures and drawings T2d to write sentences to match pictures or sequences of pictures T15 to use writing to communicate in a variety of ways, incorporating it into play and everyday classroom life	**SW:** write labels; captions; a new page. **GW:** match labels & pictures; write a label; complete a fact page; write own fruit page.
UNIT 3 **Modern Rhymes** **BB:** Alphabet Hide and Seek **PB:** Rat-a-Ta-Tat! **PB:** Days of the Week	**To find and use word patterns like rhyme and rhythm** T10 to re-read and recite rhymes with predictable and repeated patterns and experiment with similar rhyming patterns T14 to use experience of poems as a basis for independent writing, and through shared composition with adults	**SW:** write rhyming words; rules for playing a game; innovating on text. **GW:** write rhyming words; sentences to text rhythm; rhyming words; new version of poem.
UNIT 4 **Patterned Stories** **BB:** Let's Go Shopping, Little Hippo **PB:** I'm Too Scared **PB:** Yummy Honey	**To re-tell a story** T6 to re-read frequently a variety of familiar texts T7 to use knowledge of familiar texts to re-enact or re-tell to others, recounting the main points in the correct sequence T8 to locate and read significant parts of the text T9 to be aware of story structures, e.g. actions/reactions, consequences, and the ways that stories are built up and concluded T10 to re-read and recite stories and rhymes with predictable and repeated patterns and experiment with similar rhyming patterns T11f to apply knowledge of letter/sound correspondences in helping the teacher to scribe, and re-reading what the class has written T12a to experiment with writing in a variety of play, exploratory and role-play situations T12d to write sntences to match pictures or sequences of pictures T13 to think about and discuss what they intend to write, ahead of writing it	**SW:** write a new sentence about the middle of the story; a sentence about the shopping; a speech bubble for a new character. **GW:** write a sentence about the story; a speech bubble for a new character; a new ending; sentences using the same pattern.

Text types	Objectives	Writing outcomes
UNIT 5 **Recounts** **BB:** At the Weekend **PB:** In the Holidays **PB:** Last Week	**To say what has happened, in the right order** T1a to recognise printed and handwritten words in a variety of settings T1b that words can be written down to be read again for a wide range of purposes T7 to use knowledge of familiar texts to re-enact or re-tell to others, recounting the main points in correct sequence T12d to write sentences to match pictures or sequences of pictures T13 to think about and discuss what they intend to write, ahead of writing it T14 to use experience of stories, poems and simple recounts as a basis for independent writing	**SW:** write a sentence beginning 'On Saturday…', 'On Sunday…'; finish sentences: 'First…', 'Next…', 'Then…'; concluding speech bubble. **GW:** write sentences with 'I went,'; 'I saw/got…'; write a word and draw a picture for a day; write a sentence for what happened on one day.
UNIT 6 **Traditional Stories** **BB:** Chicken Licken **PB:** Sly Fox and Red Hen **PB:** Little Red Hen	**To recognise and use story language** T4 to notice the difference between spoken and written forms through re-telling known stories; to compare 'told' stories with what the book 'says' T5 to understand how story book language works and to use some formal elements when retelling stories T6 to re-read frequently a variety of familiar texts T7 to use knowledge of familiar texts to re-enact or re-tell to others, recounting the main points in correct sequence T8 to locate and read significant parts of the text T9 to be aware of story structures, e.g. actions/reactions, consequences, and the ways that stories are built up and concluded T12d to write sentences to match pictures or sequences of pictures T14 to use experience of stories, poems and simple recounts as a basis for independent writing	**SW:** write a new opening sentence; new sentences to sum up the beginning/middle/end of the story; a speech bubble for Foxy Loxy. **GW:** sequence pictures to retell the story; complete sentences to retell story using storybook language; sequence pictures to retell the story and write a sentence using storybook language; a speech bubble for the end of the story.

YEAR 1/P2 Key Objectives and Writing Outcomes

Text types	Objectives	Writing outcomes
UNIT 1 **Everyday Stories** **BB:** The Windy Washing Day **PB:** Erin's New Trainers **PB:** The Amazing School Dinners	**To know that a story has a beginning, a middle and an end** **Term 1** T3 to notice the difference between spoken and written forms through retelling known stories; compare oral versions with the written text T5 to describe story settings and incidents and relate them to own experience and that of others T7 to re-enact stories in a variety of ways T9 to write about events in personal experience linked to a variety of familiar incidents from stories T11 to make simple picture storybooks with sentences, modelling them on basic text conventions	**SW:** write a sentence about what happens at the beginning, middle and end of the story; add a new item of clothing; a new final sentence. **GW:** write instructions for making domino biscuits; for how to change a reading book; for making a piece of artwork; for how to turn on and shut down a computer.
UNIT 2 **Instructions** **BB:** How to Make and Play the Giant Snake Game **PB:** How to Make Alphabet Biscuits **PB:** How to Make a Flapping Owl	**To write instructions that tell the reader what to do and are in the right order** T13 to read and follow simple instructions T16 to write and draw simple instructions and labels for everyday classroom use	**SW:** write task cards for the game; numbered steps for playing musical statues; instructions for playing snakes and ladders. **GW:** write instructions for making domino biscuits; for how to change a reading book; for making a different piece of artwork; for how to turn on and shut down a computer.
UNIT 3 **Signs and Labels** **BB:** The Summer Fair **PB:** Our Classroom **PB:** Our School	**To give the reader information in the best way** **Term 1** T12 to read and use captions T14 to write captions for their own work T15 to make simple lists for planning, reminding, etc **Term 2** T22 to write labels for drawings and diagrams T23 to produce extended captions	**SW:** write a list of the signs and labels in the Big Book; list of rules for using a bouncy castle; extend the Big Book captions. **GW:** write a name label and label for classroom storage; a caption for the 'Child of the Day' notice; complete a school dinners notice; extended captions.
UNIT 4 **Fairy Tales** **BB:** Cinderella **PB:** The Three Wishes **PB:** The Old Woman Who Lived in a Vinegar Bottle	**To understand how fairy tales are structured, and use these structures in own writing** **Term 2** T4 to retell stories, giving the main points in sequence and to notice differences between written and spoken forms in retelling T7 to discuss reasons for, or cause of, incidents in stories T14 to represent outlines of story plots using, e.g. captions, pictures, arrows to record main incidents in order T16 to use some of the elements of known stories to structure own writing	**SW:** add simple sentences about setting and characters to the outline; write new sentences to make clear the reasons for events; speech bubbles for characters. **GW:** plot the events on a story planner; write sentences to retell the story, including reasons for events; make a story map; two speech bubbles to show a new event in the story.
UNIT 5 **Stories From Around the World** **BB:** The Queen of the Goats **PB:** Anansi and the Lion **PB:** The Magic Pine Cone	**To be able to describe a character** T5 to identify and record some key features of story language from a range of stories, and to practise reading and using them T6 to identify and discuss a range of story themes and to collect and compare T8 to identify and discuss characters; to speculate how they might behave; to discuss how they are described in the text; and to compare characters from different stories or plays T9 to become aware of character and dialogue, e.g. by role playing parts when reading aloud with others T10 to identify and compare basic story elements e.g. beginnings and endings in different stories T15 to build simple profiles of characters from stories read, describing characteristics, appearances, behaviour with pictures, single words, captions, words and sentences from text	**SW:** write words to describe the main character; collect words to describe characters and write a sentence about each; a character description. **GW:** write a character description in the form of a riddle; two contrasting character descriptions; descriptions of the main characters; a longer description of one or all of the characters.

YEAR 1/P2 Key Objectives and Writing Outcomes

Text types	Objectives	Writing outcomes
UNIT 6 **Reports** **BB:** Clothes for the Job **PB:** How Do They Keep Warm? **PB:** Barn Owls	**To use question marks properly in writing** *Term 2* T17 to use terms 'fiction' and 'non-fiction', noting some of their differing features T18 to read non fiction books and understand that the reader doesn't need to go from start to finish but selects according to what is needed T24 to write simple questions, e.g. as part of interactive display T25 to assemble information from own experience; to use simple sentences to describe, based on examples from reading T19 to predict what a given book might be about from a brief look at both front and back covers, including blurb, title, illustration; to discuss what it might tell in advance of reading and check to see if it does T21 to understand the purpose of contents pages and indexes and begin to locate information by page numbers and words by initial letter *Term 3* T19 to identify simple questions and use text to find answers. To locate parts of text that give particular information including labelled diagrams and charts T21 to use the language and features of non-fiction books to make class books T22 to write own questions prior to reading for information and to record answers	**SW:** write simple questions relating to the topic; add new sentences for the new headings; write an additional sentence. **GW:** write a heading and one sentence about Arctic foxes; an explanatory sentence; a heading and a question about barn owls; a heading and three sentences about barn owls.
UNIT 7 **Fantasy Stories** **BB:** Leo and Errol **PB:** Pass the Zapper **PB:** The Flying Bubble	**To describe a setting so that it paints a picture in the reader's mind** *Term 3* T5 to re-tell stories, to give the main points in sequence and to pick out significant incidents T6 to prepare and re-tell stories orally, identifying and using some of the more formal features of story language T8 to compare and contrast stories with a variety of settings T13 to write about significant incidents from known stories T14 to write stories using simple settings, e.g. based on previous reading	**SW:** retell the story orally and in writing; write detailed descriptions of the river and mountain settings; write a new episode for the story. **GW:** write two sentences about what it was like flying through space; a new adventure for Kim; retell the story and add descriptions of the settings to a plot flowchart; write about a new adventure for Liz and Baby Billy.
UNIT 8 **Poetry** **BB:** Late Last Night/Action Poem **PB:** All Sorts of Animals **PB:** Night Time	**To use poems as models for own writing** *Term 1* T6 to recite rhymes with predictable and repeating patterns, extemporising on patterns orally by substituting words and phrases, extending patterns, inventing patterns and playing with rhyme T10 to use rhymes and patterned stories as models for their own writing *Term 2* T11 to learn and recite simple poems and rhymes with no actions, and to re-read them from the text T13 to substitute and extend patterns from reading through language play, e.g. by using same lines and introducing new words, extending rhyming or alliterative patterns, adding further rhyming words, lines *Term 3* T9 To read a variety of poems on similar themes T10 to compare and contrast preferences and common themes in stories and poems T11 to collect class and individual favourite poems for class anthologies, participate in reading aloud T15 to use poems or parts of poems as models for own writing T16 to compose own poetic sentences, using repetitive patterns, carefully selected sentences and imagery	**SW:** add adjectives to create a new version of the poem; write some new actions; write a new verse. **GW:** write new descriptions like those in the poem; some new verses for the poem using descriptive phrases; a new version of the poem on a different theme.
UNIT 9 **Recounts** **BB:** My Visit to the Theatre **PB:** A Day in the Life of a Puppeteer **PB:** Our Puppet Week	**To use connectives to put events in order** *Term 3* T12 through shared and guided writing to apply phonological, graphic knowledge and sight vocabulary to spell words accurately T18 to read recounts and begin to recognise generic structure T20 to write simple recounts linked to topics of interest/study or to personal experience, using the language of texts read as models for own writing. Make group/class books T21 to use the language and features of non-fiction texts, e.g. captions for pictures	**SW:** write a past tensecaption to a picture; write what happened 'First...', 'At that...', 'At the end'; a closing comment. **GW:** write a past tense caption; complete sentences: 'First...', 'After lunch...', 'At the end...'; a past tense sentence using a day of the week; write a sentence about the best day of the week.using a day of the week; write a sentence about the best day of the week.

YEAR 2/P3 Key Objectives

Text types	Objectives	Writing outcomes
UNIT 1 **Everyday Stories** **BB:** The Best Ever Sleep-over **PB:** Just Like Jamie Johnson **PB:** Lost at the Theme Park	To use the language of time to write stories about familiar situations ***Term 1*** T3 to be aware of the difference between spoken and written language through comparing oral recounts with text; make use of formal story elements in re-telling T4 to understand time and sequential relationships in stories, i.e. what happened when T5 to identify and discuss reasons for events in stories, linked to plot T6 to discuss familiar story themes and link to own experiences, e.g. illness, getting lost, going away T10 to use story structure to write about own experience in same/similar form T11 to use language of time to structure a sequence of events, e.g. 'when I had finished…', 'Suddenly…', 'after that…'.	**SW:** continue the beginning of the story; write sentences for the middle of the story, using connectives; a sentence and speech bubble for the end of the story. **GW:** retell the main points of the story; complete sentences to tell a story; sentences for a story beginning (including time of year and weather); a plan for a story about getting lost in a different setting.
UNIT 2 **Instructions** **BB:** How to…Go Swimming **PB:** How to…Have Fun at the Beach **PB:** How to…Visit the Farm	To make sure my instructions are clear to the reader and in the correct order T13 to read simple written instructions, simple recipes, plans, instructions for constructing something T14 to note key structural features, e.g. clear statement of purpose at start, direct language T15 to write simple instructions, e.g. getting to school, playing a game T16 to use models from reading to organise instructions sequentially, e.g. listing points in order, each depending on the previous one, numbering T17 to use diagrams in instructions, e.g. drawing and labelling diagrams as part of a set of instructions T18 to use appropriate register in writing instructions, i.e. direct, impersonal, building on texts read	**SW:** write a simple set of directions; simple directions including key landmarks; a set of rules. **GW:** write a set of directions; instructions for how to make and play Pass the Parcel; a set of directions; instructions for making jam sandwich.
UNIT 3 **Poetry** **BB:** The World of Weird/My Home/10-Pin Bowling **PB:** Chips and Ice Cream **PB:** Dinosaur Dreams	To use poems as a model for writing ***Term 1*** T7 to learn, re-read and recite favourite poems, taking account of punctuation; to comment on aspects such as word combinations, sound patterns (such as alliterative patterns) and forms of presentation T8 to collect and categorise poems to build into class anthologies T12 to use simple poetry structures and to substitute own ideas, write new lines ***Term 2*** T8 to read own poems aloud T9 to identify and discuss patterns of rhythm, rhyme and other features of sound in different poems T10 to comment on and recognise when the reading aloud of a poem makes sense and is effective T11 to identify and discuss favourite poems and poets, using appropriate terms (poet, poem, verse, rhyme, etc.) and referring to the language of the poems T15 to use structures from poems as a basis for writing, by extending or substituting elements, inventing own lines, verses; to make class collections, illustrate with captions; to write own poems from initial jottings and words ***Term 3*** T6 to read, respond imaginatively, recommend and collect examples of humorous poems T8 to discuss meanings of words and phrases that create humour, and sound effects in poetry, e.g. nonsense poems, tongue-twisters, riddles, and to classify poems into simple types; to make class anthologies T11 to use humorous verse as a structure for children to write their own by adaptation, mimicry or substitution; to invent own riddles, language puzzles, jokes, nonsense sentences etc derived from reading; write tongue twisters, alliterative sentences; select words with care, re-reading and listening to their effect	**SW:** write sentences in the style of the last two lines of the poem; alliterative sentences; a new verse. **GW:** write another poem based on *Red*; a new version of the poem; a new poem with a similar structure; a new version of the poem.
UNIT 4 **Traditional Stories** **BB:** The First Sunrise **PB:** How the Finches Got Their Colours **PB:** How the Turtle Got His Shell	***Term 2*** To use traditional stories as a model for writing T3 to discuss and compare story themes T4 to predict story endings/incidents, e.g. from unfinished extracts, while reading with the teacher T5 to discuss story settings; to compare differences; to locate key words and phrases in text; to consider how different settings influence events and behaviour T6 to identify and describe characters, expressing own views and using words and phrases from text	**SW:** extend the description of the setting and characters; plan a new story based on the setting and structure of the Big Book; write the opening of a new traditional story based on the Big Book. **GW:** write a character sketch/plot outline for the main characters; a character sketch/plot

Text types	Objectives	Writing outcomes
Unit 4 continued	T7 to prepare and re-tell stories individually and through role-play in groups, using dialogue and narrative from text T13 to use story settings from reading, e.g. re-describe, use in own writing, write a different story in the same setting T14 to write character profiles, e.g. simple descriptions, posters, passports, using key words and phrases that describe or are spoken by characters in the text	outline for a new story; a character/plot outline for Turtle; a character/plot outline for a new character and story.
UNIT 5 **Dictionaries** **BB:** Dictionary of Games and Sports **PB:** Amazing Dictionary of Hats **PB:** Glorious Gloves Dictionary	**To put dictionary entries in alphabetical order and ensure that definitions are clear to the reader** T16 to use dictionaries and glossaries to locate words by using initial letter T17 that dictionaries and glossaries give definitions and explanations; discuss what definitions are T18 to use other alphabetically ordered texts, e.g. indexes, directories, listings, registers; to discuss how they are used T20 to make class dictionaries and glossaries of special interest words, giving explanations and definitions, e.g. linked to topics derived from stories and poems	**SW:** add new games and sports to the Big Book in the correct place; write a new definition; new entries for the glossary. **GW:** put items in alphabetical order and write a definition; definitions for a group dictionary of shoes; new definitions and glossary for the dictionary of gloves; definitions and glossary for a group dictionary
UNIT 6 **Explanations** **BB:** What is Recycling? **PB:** Why Does...? **PB:** Tell Me Why...	**To ask and answer questions to explain why or how something happens and to use flow diagrams in explanations** T19 to read flow charts and cyclical diagrams that explain a process T21 to produce simple flow charts or diagrams that explain a process	**SW:** captions for photographs in the Big Book; a flow diagram for the paper recycling process; a flow diagram about the use of paper at school. **GW:** write an answer to a question from the book; a flow diagram to explain why water boils; a flow diagram about how a torch works; an explanation of the life cycle of a tree.
UNIT 7 **Different Stories by the Same Author** **BB:** Alan MacDonald **PB:** Yummy Scrummy **PB:** The Cleaner Genie	***Term 3*** **To make sure a story has a beginning, a middle with at least two events, a problem and an ending** T4 to compare books by same author: settings, characters, themes; to evaluate and form preferences, giving reasons T10 to write sustained stories, using their knowledge of story elements: narrative, settings, characterisation, dialogue and the language of story	**SW:** plan a story; complete a story plan; develop the middle of a story. **GW:** make a plan of the story; complete a character study; make a plan of the story and make notes comparing two texts; write a sustained story.
UNIT 8 **Reports** **BB:** What's Under the Road? **PB:** A Look Around a Log **PB:** Inside a Rock Pool	**To use notes to help with planning. To organise writing so it is clear to the reader** T14 to pose questions and record these in writing, prior to reading non fiction to find answers T15 to use a contents page and index to find way about text T16 to scan a text to find specific sections, e.g. key words and phrases, subheadings T17 to skim or read title, contents page, illustrations, chapter headings, etc., to speculate what a book might be about T18 to evaluate the usefulness of a text for its purpose T19 to make simple notes from non-fiction texts, e.g. key words, phrases, page references, headings, to use in subsequent writing T20 to write non-fiction texts, using texts read as models for own writing, e.g. use of headings, sub-headings, captions T21 to write non-chronological reports based on the structure of known texts, e.g. 'There are 2 sorts of...; They live in...; The As have x but the Bs...etc., using appropriate language to present, sequence and categorise ideas	**SW:** make spider diagram to show content/structure of the text; new page for shared text; another new page for shared text. **GW:** make spidergram to show organisation of part of text; plan for new section of book and the opening part of next section; spidergram to show organisation of part of text; new section for the book, and opening part of the new section.
UNIT 9 **Stories by Significant Authors** **BB:** Book Reviews and Blurbs **PB:** Charlie and the Cart **PB:** A Sheepless Night	**To write author profiles, book reviews and book blurbs, and back up opinions with reference to the text** T5 to read about authors from information on book covers, e.g. other books written, whether author is alive or dead, publisher; to become aware of authorship and publication T7 to compare books by different authors on similar themes; to evaluate, giving reasons T12 to write simple evaluations of books read and discussed giving reasons	**SW:** write a blurb for a known story; an author profile; a book review. **GW:** write a book blurb for Charlie and the Cart; a book review including comparison of two stories; a book blurb and a book review; a comparison of the two Guided Writing texts.

LEVELLING CHARTS

These charts show:

■ The corresponding level of ORT to the particular pupil book. Please note that these stages are a guide only and cannot be exact.

■ The average number of words per page. Please note that is an average figure. For lower level books, there will be a consistent number of words on each page; for higher levels, there will be differing levels of text on each page.

■ Features which affect the level of difficulty: this includes features which help keep the reading level low, as well as features that might make the text more challenging. There is also a list of all the particular text features of each book (eg coloured text, exclamation marks, onomatopoeia, charts etc) to give you an at-a-glance look at the content. This is designed to aid you in your choice of book for the ability of your group, and also to enable you to see which text features you may wish to point out to the children.

Levelling in Guided Writing Books RECEPTION/P1

Title	ORT	Words pp	Features that affect level of difficulty
UNIT 1: Nursery Rhymes			
Ring-a-Ring-a-Roses	1+	4	● Familiar rhyme, repetition, high level of predictability. ● Coloured font, different sized fonts, dashes, exclamation mark, comma, 'animated' text for emphasis.
Polly Puts the Kettle On	2	9	● Word count increase is mostly due to repeated phrases; new vocabulary can be guessed from pictures. ● Alliteration, contractions: we'll, it's; comma; exclamation mark.
UNIT 2: Information Books			
Colours	1+	7	● Nouns in titles will need help from adult but all other nouns are illustrated. ● Non-fiction features: contents, index, heading, label; individual words written vertically.
Inside a Fruit	2	14	● Title word is illustrated. First sentence always states colour. Repetition of 'It feels' and 'It has'. ● Non-fiction features: contents, index, heading, label, captions; text presented on a variety of positions; complete sentences with variety of adjectives.
UNIT 3: Modern Rhymes			
Rat-a-Ta-Tat!	1+	5	● Repetition and rhyme give high level of predictability. ● Text in a variety of different positions, white text on coloured background, dream bubble; contraction – it's; exclamation mark; onomatopoeia: meow.
Days of the Week	2	4	● Day of the week is predictable. New word in the sentence can be worked out from first phoneme. ● Shaded and coloured text, individual words in non-standard font and speech bubble; variety of positions of text; environmental print including capital letters; exclamation mark.

Title	ORT	Words pp	Features that affect level of difficulty
UNIT 4: Patterned Stories			
I'm Too Scared	2	12	● CVC words; Ben, top, fun; six word sentence is repeated on nearly every page.
			● One setting, range of characters, predictable ending; speech marks; non-standard speech bubble as part of text; contraction: I'm, exclamation mark; onomatopoeia.
Yummy Honey	3	9	● Phrase from one page is repeated on the next.
			● Coloured text; variety of positions for text, text in capital letters for emphasis, exclamation marks – several used at one time for emphasis; contractions: that's, I'll; speech marks; speech bubble; onomatopoeia.
UNIT 5: Recount			
In the Holidays	2	5	● 'new' and 'watched' are the only words that are not either high frequency or illustrated by the picture.
			● Title in coloured font, text in 'hand written' font on different coloured strips, text in different 'voices' with photograph of 'speaker', postcards and 'real' objects.
Last Week	3	7	● CVC words: had, did; new vocabulary: masks, teacher, assembly, first, everyone, clapped.
			● Text in various positions, coloured text to highlight recount structure, 'hand written' font for text, text as captions in photo album format, environmental print.
UNIT 6: Traditional Stories			
Sly Fox and Red Hen	3	10	● CVC words: back, den, fox, got, had, hen, his, nap, pot, ran, red, sack, set. Lots of high frequency and CVC words. Upper end of stage 2 as there are some longer sentences.
			● Title, author, publisher's logo; story book language, two contrasting characters, range of settings, definite sequence; exclamation mark, ellipses, onomatopoeia – Splash!
Little Red Hen	4	15	● CVC words: but, did, hen, mill, not, red, will. Lots of repetition, but story told through combination of text and speech bubbles.
			● Story book language, number of diverse characters, different settings; patterned language and repetitive chant; speech bubble, exclamation mark, question mark, comma, ellipse.

Levelling in Guided Writing Books YEAR 1/P2

Title	ORT	Words pp	Features that affect level of difficulty
UNIT 1: Everyday Stories Erin's New Trainers	4	9	● Most difficult words are 'trainers' and 'backpack' (illustrated). 'Purple', 'stripy' and 'shiny' are all illustrated by the word presented. Otherwise familiar vocabulary.
The Amazing School Dinners	5	18	● Speech bubbles; speech marks, question marks, hyphenated words, text in a variety of positions on the page. ● Most sentences have connectives, 'and', 'but', 'so' or time related links, e.g. 'Another day...' Pictures will help children to predict the text. Most difficult words are: different, sausages, spaghetti, special. ● Contraction, ellipses, exclamation marks; text in a variety of positions on page; text as part of an illustration.
UNIT 2: Instructions How to make Alphabet Biscuits	4	8	● Instructions can be deduced from the pictures. Most difficult words: ingredients, different, coloured, tablespoon, sieve, squeeze. ● Varying page layout, short sentences beginning with verbs, text in a variety of positions including vertically, numbers.
How to make a Flapping Owl	5	14	● Most of the instructions are clear from the pictures. Most difficult words: scissors, fasteners, decorate. ● Varying page layout, short sentences beginning with verbs, text in a variety of positions including vertically, numbers.
UNIT 3: Signs and Labels Our Classroom	4	15	● Word count is raised by list of days and months on page 9. Labels are in familiar wording. Most difficult words are: welcome, classroom, quietly, polite, remember. ● Text in headings, captions, labels, notices, etc., text in variety of positions, fonts, sizes & colours, text in columns.
Our School	5	15	● Page 5 has most words, but ideas will be familiar. Most difficult words are: remember, marracas, gato drums, tambourines, strictly. Notices in other languages. ● Text in headings, captions, labels, notices, etc., different languages written in range of scripts, text in variety of positions, fonts, sizes & colours, text in columns.
UNIT 4: Fairy Tales The Three Wishes	5	19	● Longer sentences with 'and', 'but' and 'so'. Pictures support prediction. Most difficult words: woodcutter, sausage.
The Old Woman Who Lived in a Vinegar Bottle	6	29	● High average word count, but repeated phrases and format make it easier. Speech bubbles break up the text. Most difficult words: vinegar, grumbled, mumble, surprised.
UNIT 5: Stories From Around the World Anansi and the Lion	5	14	● Familiar vocabulary. Hardest words are: Anansi, squeaked. ● Speech marks, exclamation marks, possessive apostrophe.
The Magic Pine Cone	6	24	● Most difficult words: daughter, thousand, whispered. Pictures support child in predicting what happened next. ● Speech marks, exclamation marks, possessive apostrophe, hyphen, ellipses, contraction.

Levelling in Guided Writing Books YEAR 1/P2

Title	ORT	Words pp	Features that affect level of difficulty
UNIT 6: Reports			
How Do They Keep Warm?	4	15	● Repetition of 'They have... to keep them warm.' Most difficult words: Arctic, Antarctic, blubber. ● Non-fiction features: contents and index with more than one entry per letter, map. Text in a variety of positions on the page.
Barn Owls	5	16	● No repetition. Mostly simple sentences. Most difficult words: pellet, buildings. ● Non-fiction features: contents and index with more than one entry per letter, headings, labels, technical vocabulary. Text in a variety of positions on the page.
UNIT 7: Fantasy Stories			
Pass the Zapper	4	12	● Only one or two sentences per page but quite a lot of new vocabulary. Most difficult words: zapper, afternoon, pointed, television. ● Speech marks, exclamation marks, text in a variety of different positions, colours, sizes and fonts including enlarged.
The Flying Bubble	5	18	● Mostly simple sentences. Longer sentences with 'but' have repeated phrase. Most difficult words: dinosaurs, swooping, spiky, bounced, through. ● Speech marks, exclamation marks, onomatopoeia; text in a variety of different positions, colours, sizes and fonts including enlarged.
UNIT 8: Poetry			
All Sorts of Animals	4	21	● Lots of repetition in each poem. Rhyme helps predict words. Pictures illustrate new nouns, e.g. dinosaur, monster. ● Most difficult words: clucked, grunted, bellowed, through, scratches, scuttles, wriggles.
Night Time	5	18	● Mostly list poems. Children can use the pictures to predict nouns. Most difficult words: scrumpled, pyjamas, rhinos, thunder, daggers, breathing.
UNIT 9: Recounts			
A Day in the Life of a Puppeteer	5	15	● Most sentences have connectives related to time. Photos show order of events. Longest sentence has 13 words. Most difficult words: puppeteer, storeroom, theatre, afterwards.
Our Puppet Week	6	17	● Most sentences have connectives related to time. Photos show the order of events. Longest sentence has 12 words. ● Most difficult words: afterwards, decided, theatre, different.

Levelling in Guided Writing Books YEAR 2/P3

Title	ORT	Words pp	Features that affect level of difficulty
UNIT 1: Everyday Stories Just Like Jamie Johnson	7	34	• Mostly simple sentences. Some connectives, e.g. 'One winter morning,' 'After school'.
			• Story with a series of events and two main characters; text in a variety of positions and fonts including enlarged print; dialogue sequences, range of punctuation including speech marks, ellipses, hyphen, possessive apostrophe, alliteration, contractions.
Lost at the Theme Park	7	38	• Some longer sentences but familiar situation. New vocabulary can be predicted from the pictures.
			• Story with a range of characters, predictable structure and ending. Text in a variety of positions and fonts including enlarged print, environmental print and within an illustration; dialogue sequences; speech bubbles, thought bubbles; range of punctuation including speech marks, exclamation marks, question marks, contractions.
UNIT 2: Instructions How to... Have Fun at the Beach	7	25	• Talking about the map will introduce new nouns, e.g. parade, kiosk. Instructions are in single sentences. Pictures of the game illustrate most difficult words, e.g. 'stretched,' 'crawling'.
			• Range of instructions including directions and rules, wide variety of imperatives. Non-fiction features: contents, index, headings, numbered points; text in a variety of positions including in panels and captions, in a range of different fonts, colours and sizes.
How to...Visit the Farm	8	33	• Directions and recipes may have two sentences. Readers will be helped to predict by referring to the pictures and by following the map. Most difficult words are: respect, liquid, container, separate, moisture.
			• Range of instructions including directions and rules, wide variety of imperatives. Non-fiction features: contents, index, headings, sub-headings, labels, captions, numbered points, bullet points, charts, abbreviations; text in a variety of positions including in panels and captions, in a range of different fonts, colours and sizes.
UNIT 3: Poetry Chips and Ice Cream	6	36	• Hardest words: shrieked, programmes, mushrooms, breadfruit.
			• Different layout of text and illustration on every page related to the type of poem & including range of fonts and bold & enlarged text; range of rhymes with same/similar spelling patterns; range of punctuation including speech marks, exclamations marks, colon, question marks, commas.
Dinosaur Dreams	7	52	• High average word count, but most poems have rhymes, e.g. Blue, Slick Nick's Dog's Tricks, have more predictability. Hardest poem is Dinosaur Dream Recipe: 'prehistoric', 'quality', 'landscape', 'imagination'.
			• Different layout of text and illustration on every page related to the type of poem and including range of fonts , bold & enlarged words, use of capitals for emphasis. Range of rhymes including same/similar spelling patterns and different spellings, alliterations, onomatopoeia; range of punctuation including speech marks, exclamation marks, colon, question marks, commas; contractions, possessive apostrophe.
UNIT 4: Traditional Stories How the Finches Got Their Colours	7	25	• Most pages have only two sentences. Longest sentence has 20 words (10 of which have 3 letters or fewer). Most difficult words: beautiful, screeched, prettiest.
			• Traditional storybook language, and clear structure with obvious beginning, middle and end; text in a variety of positions on page & in different colours and fonts, dialogue between characters that carried the story. Wide range of punctuation; most pages have only two sentences.
How the Turtle Got His Shell	8	29	• Most sentences are compound sentences with 'when', 'so', 'but' 'if', 'one day', etc. Longest sentence has 22 words (10 of which have 3 letters or fewer). Most difficult words: Binama, hornbill, necklaces, bracelets, already.
			• Traditional story-book language and clear structure with obvious beginning, middle and end. Text in a variety of positions on page and in different colours and fonts; dialogue between characters that carried the story; wide range of punctuation.

Title		ORT	Words pp	Features that affect level of difficulty
UNIT 5: Dictionaries				
	Amazing Dictionary of Hats	8	42	• Most sentences are short. Most difficult words: invented, skateboarders, synthetic, fictional, traditional, yarmulke. Glossary explains words such as Sikh, Morocco . • Non-fiction features: alphabet, headings, sub headings, glossary, pronunciation guide, dates; page layout and language related to definitions.
	Glorious Gloves Dictionary	9	45	• Most difficult words: synthetic, falconer, detergent, welder are listed with definitions in the glossary. • Non-fiction features: headings, sub-headings, glossary, brackets, more than one entry for same letter; groups of letters at top of page; page layout and language related to definitions.
UNIT 6: Explanations				
	Why Does....	8	47	• Sentences are mostly short statements, but ideas may be new, e.g. 'Materials that are lighter than water float.' Most difficult words are: temperature, materials, geyser. • Non-fiction features: contents, index, headings, sub-headings, labels, chart, numbers; text in a wide variety of positions, fonts, sizes and colours.
	Tell Me Why...?	9	51	• Most sentences are short, but child needs the vocabulary to understand them, e.g. 'A torch is powered by electricity.' Most difficult words are: reproduce, life cycle, chemicals, circuit, electricity. • Non-fiction features: contents, index, glossary, headings, sub headings, labels, chart, diagram, cross section numbers; text in a wide variety of positions, fonts, sizes and colours.
UNIT 7: Different Stories by the Same Author				
	Yummy Scrummy	8	48	• Lots of high frequency words. Quite easy to predict that will happen next. Longest sentence is 25 words (11 of which have 3 letters or fewer). Mostly simple sentences or compound sentences with 'and', 'if' 'so' or 'but'. • Hardest words: chocolate, treasure, radiator. Text highlights to show the structure of the story.
	The Cleaner Genie	9	68	• Conversation on nearly every page. Longest sentence is 19 words. Mostly simple sentences, or compound sentences with 'and', 'but' or 'so'. Hardest words: completely, realised, avalanche, vacuum. Text highlights to show the structure of the story.
UNIT 8: Reports				
	A Look Around a Log	8	24	• Mostly short sentences. Longest is 15 words (of which have 3 letters or fewer). Hardest words: amphibians, larvae, centipedes. • Non-fiction features: contents, index with several entries for same letter, glossary, headings, sub-headings, labels, diagram; formal language of classification.
	Inside a Rock Pool	9	53	• One long paragraph (72 words). Information text, so not easy to predict what comes next. Most difficult words are: barnacles, anemones, plankton, tentacles, creatures. • Non-fiction features: contents, index with several entries for same letter, glossary, headings, sub-headings, captions, labels, diagrams including life cycle; formal language of classification.
UNIT 9: Stories by Significant Authors				
	Charlie and the Cart by Martin Waddell	8	55	• Lots of high frequency words. Mostly short sentences; the longest is 22 words. Chapter headings. Hardest words: ellipses, solving. Story with six main characters and a surprise ending. Lots of dialogue, some thought bubbles, lots of ellipses and use of storybook language, with text in brackets to indicate what the animals are trying to say. Text bubbles to show two readers' comments.
	A Sheepless Night by Geraldine McCaughrean	9	65	• Mostly short sentences. Chapter headings. Hardest words: likeable, character, view, judge. Story with one main character and a surprising animal situation. Mainly short sentences. Sometimes challenging vocabulary and lots of dialogue. Text bubbles to show two readers' comments on the book.

Correlations to English 5–14 (National Guidelines for Scotland)

Coverage for P1

Text type	Level	Attainment targets/programme of study
UNIT 1 **Nursery Rhymes**	A	Spelling: an interest in words, how they sound, how they are made. Knowledge about language: letter, word.
UNIT 2 **Information Books**	A	Functional writing: teacher will help select important features and act as scribe. Knowledge about language: letter, word, capital.
UNIT 3 **Modern Rhymes**	A	Spelling: an interest in words, how they sound, how they are made.
UNIT 4 **Patterned Stories**	A	Imaginative writing: teacher will develop children's awareness of sequence. Personal writing: help children speak confidently about themselves.
UNIT 5 **Recounts**	A	Personal writing: children will express ideas through drawings. When pupils first compose, their stories may consist of single sentences.
UNIT 6 **Traditional Stories**	A	Imaginative writing: a character or animal becomes a focus for imagined events. Knowledge about language: letter, word.

Coverage for P2

Text type	Level	Attainment targets/programme of study
UNIT 1 **Everyday Stories**	A	Imaginative writing: teacher can develop awareness of sequence by looking at beginnings, middles and endings. Knowledge about language: letter, word, sentence, capital, full stop.
UNIT 2 **Instructions**	A	Functional writing: sequence can be explored using drawings. Teacher will help pupils to order their writing and act as scribe. Knowledge about language: letter, word, sentence, capital, full stop.
UNIT 3 **Signs and Labels**	A	Functional writing: pupils will report orally to the teacher and to others. Teacher will help pupils to observe, to select important features, to order their writing and act as scribe.
UNIT 4 **Fairy Tales**	A	Imaginative writing: teacher will stimulate excitement and enthusiasm for writing. A character may become the focus for imagined events. Role-play and expressive activities can be starting points for imaginative explorations.
UNIT 5 **Stories From Around the World**	A	Imaginative writing: teacher will stimulate excitement and enthusiasm for writing. A character or animal may become the focus for imagined events. Role-play and expressive activities can be starting points for imaginative explorations.
UNIT 6 **Reports**	A	Functional writing: pupils will report orally to teacher and to others. Teacher will help pupils to observe, to select important features, to order their writing and act as scribe.
UNIT 7 **Fantasy Stories**	A	Imaginative writing: teacher will stimulate excitement and enthusiasm for writing. A character or animal may become the focus for imagined events. Role-play and expressive activities can be starting points for imaginative explorations.

Text type	Level	Attainment targets/programme of study
UNIT 8 **Poetry**	A	Spelling: pupils should be given an interest in words, how they sound, how they are made and the patterns within them. Emphasis will be on enjoyment, centred on their own writing and reading.
UNIT 9 **Recounts**	A	Personal writing: teacher will discuss, decide with the children the main points, act as scribe. When pupils first compose their own stories may consist of single sentences. This can be aided by the provision of printed words and phrases for story-making.

Coverage for P3

Text type	Level	Attainment targets/programme of study
UNIT 1 **Everyday Stories**	B	Imaginative writing: teacher will help children draft what they wish to say, by questioning, giving a model, and discussing appropriate vocabulary. Punctuation and structure: pupils will begin to identify the need for capital letters and full stops to establish meaning.
UNIT 2 **Instructions**	B	Functional writing: pupils will use simple notes to order their writing. Teacher will make pupils aware of different styles and demonstrate layout features.
UNIT 3 **Poetry**	B	Imaginative writing: poetry writing depends on wide experience of listening to and reading poems with discussion of structures and effects. At this stage content, rhythm and vocabulary are more important than rhyme.
UNIT 4 **Traditional Stories**	B	Imaginative writing: teacher will draw pupils' attention to aspects of story, e.g. plot, character, dialogue, setting.
UNIT 5 **Dictionaries**	B	Functional writing: pupils will use simple notes to order their writing. Teacher will make pupils aware of different styles, vocabulary suitable for different audiences and demonstrate layout features.
UNIT 6 **Explanations**	B	Functional writing: pupils will use simple notes to order their writing. Teacher will make pupils aware of different styles and demonstrate layout features.
UNIT 7 **Different Stories by the Same Author**	B C	Imaginative writing: teacher will draw pupils' attention to aspects of the story they know from reading, e.g. plot, character, dialogue and setting. Functional writing: reports based on children's reading will involve the teacher in helping them to analyse the text and identify important data.
UNIT 8 **Reports**	B	Functional writing: pupils use simple notes to order their writing. Teacher will make pupils aware of different styles, vocabulary suitable for different audiences and demonstrate layout features.
UNIT 9 **Stories by Significant Authors**	B C	Imaginative writing: teacher will draw pupils' attention to aspects of the story they know from reading, e.g. plot, character, dialogue and setting. Functional writing: reports based on children's reading will involve the teacher in helping them to analyse the text and identify important data.

GLOSSARY

guided writing: where children make decisions, compose and revise their own texts, with close support from the teacher. This is done in groups of around six children, grouped by ability level.

independent writing: where children write independently without any support from the teacher. Support may be provided through PCMs / writing frames / word banks, etc.

individual whiteboards: small, dry-wipe boards for use by children during shared and guided writing sessions

paired talk: where children discuss questions or decisions with a partner before feeding back to the teacher

PCMs: an abbreviation for photocopy masters (sometimes also known as photocopiable sheets / blackline masters)

plenary: a 'summing up' session where teachers can ask questions to gather assessment information about pupils' progress against a specific objective. This can be done at the end of a literacy hour, or, as a shorter 'summary session', at the end of a separate teaching session (eg for guided writing).

shared writing: whole class sessions where the teacher demonstrates specific aspects of the writing process

stimulus ideas: activities and questions to support the context, knowledge and understanding of a text or text type, prior to doing some writing

supported composition: where children do some of the shared writing activity. This is sometimes done in pairs, and can be done on the teacher's dry-wipe board or electronic whiteboard, or on individual dry-wipe boards.

talk for writing: where the teacher stimulates discussion to clarify children's ideas, prior to a writing activity

teacher demonstration: where the teacher controls the writing and shows children how to construct a text

teacher scribe: where children verbally compose some or all of the text, whilst the teacher refines their ideas and writes for them

writing frames: visual and textual structures which help to support effective writing

writing outcome: the writing that will be produced by the teacher and/or children by the end of a session